1

# The Accused

# A Poetry Anthology
# by
# Akaash Rishi

Published January 2023

3

*For my brother, Ritesh. Thank you.*

5

# Contents

7

I want to know what Buddhas knew

(buddhas)

To see if they fit in?...

Are they part of the world today?

Can I know what another knows?

Semblance and mimesis

When the Time is seen through

And the messy mind is laid out

For all the world to see

Beyond Israel Sharon TV

Jerusalem was -→ A.B.C.#whatcanIbe

Buttons

& mistakes in misty mountains

Happy mornings after Samaritans.

# Comic Girl

There came to pass a fateful day

That spacemen found themselves down Cornwall way,

Oh! To launch into space after the race was settled

And get through the bushy process without too many nettles.

Bringing this matter to life @Realism

Was not easy.

Lemon squeezy and you'll feel at ease "Soldier!"

The page is not the thing

The routine watch is what cold water brings

In the meantime what can we see but some bought news

And even a comedy of errors about vanity's blessings and blues.

# First Political

Turning up for campaigns
Being a pain in the class
Social distinctions are draining
The visage of togetherness fast.
It's all I can do, deliver leaflets
While they talk about political spin
And listen to the familiar faces
Contemptuous of all that social din.
Saturdays in the morning, a half past 10
I'll be there again and again
But above that line I do not cross
In case the MP shows who is the boss?
Conservative, Tory the race is narrow
The Liberals are not so democratic today
And if by Hendrix, Vishnu is so important
Then he can explain why the message is gay.
Delivery and Romans, ignore it
The omens in the imagination
The thickest sentence of my prison so far
To walkabout Northfield with leaflet in hand
And be a passenger for coffee without my own car.

# On the Padded Cell

(Ring. Ring.)

They drove me mad
It was first gear
They were all I had
That was secondary fears.
Scanned and locked
Banned and fucked.
The memory issue was only solved
By going forward in reverse.
That was a very merry hearse;
Marry me tomorrow to the lady in white
May we be the Am Japa Bunnies
Maybe it is the wedding cake
Mistakes have been made
In and outside of M-An-Hat=Tan

(Ring. Ring.)

Stopped by Jersey for a tan
Caught up with the NHS boy for some fab fans
Offline printer
Online winters
Said plaid plans for old age
Road rage
Whitsun Weddings
-> Flotsam and Jesters
Still Larkin around, I see
::-> some people should be paid for padded cell poetry
To,
Brighten Up Your Jig
and make you dance with the wig
Yours,
Tories too and their Techno game.

For parties in parks
Sex on the brain.

(Ring. Ring.)

What happened?
Spin the polity
Rave the menagerie
Meditate the meditators
Medicate and like the locating lactators
Convene the meetings at 3 o'clock
Suck on that chicken for evening sticks and sticks that won't break my bones
When your words on my dinner plate hurt me…
Wages and costs
Living on the box:
What was the (real)?
When wages were all I could feel.

(click)

# Pandemic

Out of the single market

They never saw it coming

The jokes of the Jester

Were waiting without warning.

Lost tribes

Collective blindness

The nations lost their role

Condemnation and death tolls.

Nineteen over eighteen

Corona over Karuna

The viruses spread like Kryptonite

Weakness to very SWOT team

Gordon's dream

Ginn and tunics

Emergency times

The hospitals swabbed double time

This thought is not anymore.

Sometime before Ukraine

Waiting for the pain

Lockdown and all those people at home

Gardening with new purchases

Garden gnomes

Recycle grass

This is some of the way I saw the world come to pass.

How about you?

# Puddle

Definitive
**Conclusive**
A past of its own
Sunlight betrothed
Evaporated silk
Surrounded
Others keep the master design happy
Muddy waters
Sludgy grass
tyres
tracks
Hemways and drivethroughs
Trodden down hindrances
No clear path
Complete blockage on the pavement!
{M.U.D.D.eeeeee to see}
Things you cannot see
Like the others. Undated and undertimed.

Only this one is different
Surrounded and suffocated
Others won't not be differentiated from it
A little water here
Some rotten patterns over there.
The threat of some bloated shoes
Moody moody goody two few
- > "The People Go Around It"
( a Celebrity in its own right)
One metre fine
Ten Yen and it's too far for you to jump
An adrenaline rush
A collective hatred for splashes
The minds' raving
And one the whole path wide.

Scattered remains of my hope for peace
Pieces of the land flooded
Arranged in a way that Yahweh absorbs the flesh

With the one that is unusually whole
The whole footpath long
"So long!"
I won't sing the song
Of often skipping over puddles
Drowning in the Sea Shanties.

Until I tell you how drove me mad:
"I just have to try it!"

Like a solid cattle
Pride
Prodded
Krishna drove the stampede across
To walk around
Balance!

The sheep had to come.

## <u>The World is One Team</u>

Yoga
Infinity
the bells are within me
Time
Centrality
It's too soon for superficiality
Motions
Markets
Marrakesh
Crashing
What is the use of balancing on one leg?
Behind
Above
It's different to chemicals in the Square Peg
Affront
Comfortableness
Special socks aren't needed on the mat
Above
Below
There's enough Qi for the men in a top hat
Aroundabout
Within
These classes are selling out fast
Apart
Together
Chances are I'll be leaving lessons last.

Time for a special chat with the teacher
Apples and iPads he can't try any harder
To get away from me if I am Jack Reacher
All action and no guns blazing to ongoing further.

# Intra Action

"What's your pretty poetry about Shree?"
There are things I'd like to see
City living
Corporate misgivings
Charitable livings
And the interaction between people and things.

These are then the massive movements of subsidiaries
But this is not on my level and has nothing to do with me.

**{Victim}**

# Sharing

Come to me

I am the one you want to be with

We are tortured in immortality

Tonight is our fame for the others.

We are drinkers and socialisers

Masters of the world and leaders:

We have leaned on others

Taken their deeds

Vampires and werewolves

Gothic counterparts of the imagination of tomorrow.

The morning has not yet arisen

The moon is dark and unlit by perfection.

Hades has not hostility to the awareness amongst us

As we party at the mercy of others

- *The(y) went to social advancement.*

That's what I meant,

When I was all about soul

And Billy Joel's goal.

Taking some time and a fortnight to respond

To the lady's text from the bar;

We're not going far…

…

I can't see (sometimes) the passive aggressive

Agrarian relational

Important spatials

Fractal imperials

The power, the presence and the positive…

…

How will the future affect me

Social insecurity

Wine, women and wanting

How am I offside with Ricky Ponting?

Know what I mean about the slang slide

Poet with the right to elide and glide

Not meaning to be rude

Jude the Intruder

Someone border me off, please

(I stick to praying on my knees).

# The Bonfire of the Logicians

Vulnerable

Under the table

Over and out

The child gangs are about.

Bonfires of legislators

Sufis of sweet sounds

Vibrations

Improved damages

London has carriages

Sounds of the nation

The old Vikings

The new televisions

Visions & visionaries

Drugs Cartels

Newsletters with spells

The police that chase people down

The daily bugle with more noise around town.

**The grandfather that frowns**.

PMQs and furious speeches

As far as the worries reach.

All is one and too much

Nice touch

Kick ball and bollocks all

Connection : ->

Phalluses and erections

Architecture

Geopolitical protections

How can this be when both sides are heard

Only when the nation offers offices without the herd.

"You feel it too?..."

Like sitting on the loo

It's something we all do:

Stare at what we have or had in common.

Sit and talk to the TV

Mine is not one with 4 Channels

My father is on no Government panel

My grandmother is no model for Chanel.

Can you make her messages go faster?

The Incas are linking on Al Jazeera

Some revered respect

Indigenous rejections

False acceptance

When soaps are used to wash my airs

Opulent with expectations and indecent affairs.


The mind collapses each night before angels

To, Sleep, With Love

I hope I get better and things improve soon.

Yours sincerely, the voices in the room -

Under stars adrift with Satellites of love

Bearing our news for all our Teachers

In schools like beacons for children's soundbites.

It's not easy without Priests

Negotiating country

Navigation

Supportive nation

And respect those wages in the USA

"What do you say?"

Something is a little muse under the weather.


Which conversation do you imagine?

What is the right owned tone of townsman's voice?

It depends on the millennia and who has all but gone

And let none of it remind you, you had no choice.

# The Accused

You accused me of talking

My lips were closed

Your mind was moving

The images were comfortable offers

Social occasions

Ethnic cleansing

Multicultural views

Bilateral decisions

Familiar distress

Reaching for my eyes

Leaving me lonely downhill

Falling down the stairwell

Where I am too busy on LinkedIn to be better than I am today.

# Mixed Diaspora

Sitting around the Union
Trading ideas like simple students
From all corners of the globe
Except authentically from Africa
      the Wigger in the room
      the Witch with the assistant's broom
There was so much ahead of us
Not so empty behind us
We had only 8 weeks to kill
Before Time murdered our hearts and our ideas.

Keep a light on for my Iranian comrade
So outsourced he keeps coming back to me
New Age English
I (am) afraid too much, my fiendish friend, by you and yours'
Mathematical Degree
How about the Biologist next to you
What do you expect me to do?
But freeze for the batteries for Aziz, please.

It's time to come to The Lord of The Rings
And see us children move on with Bling
And a word a day from the absent and not
counted for.
In darkness and in light
For sickness that is other people's wealth:
Keep the trade coming from Graduates in Union
Ions
days plenty
For more than sixty year olds who knew each other when they were
twenty.

# I'm Telling You Fa(r)ther

I'm telling you father

The closer you come

Your waves crash in the sea

That spaceship is following me

Against all of my regrets

You've seen the L.E.D.

And you're telling me what to do

In case of Mandirs that remain closed

Past their COVID sell by date

Of being pre-approved

Advertise advice from a lonely Jew

The farther away I get I can see

Hats that are surreptitiously meant for me

And you advise me of life and death

With your newborn Holy Ghost and heavenly breath

So, keep your distance so it's fair to see

What's going on between you and me

And I can tell when you advance

To take advantage of Kali and Kala for your only chance.

# Madness

All in good time
When the history is bad
Of Theosophical wandering
Cloudy with gold
Traders who were bold
Declarations of intention
Yogic inventions
Classical Christianity at last.

29

Printed in Great Britain
by Amazon

21332227R00020